LIGHTNING
BOLT
BOOKS™

The
Hoover
Dam

Jeffrey Zuehlke

Lerner Publications Company
Minneapolis

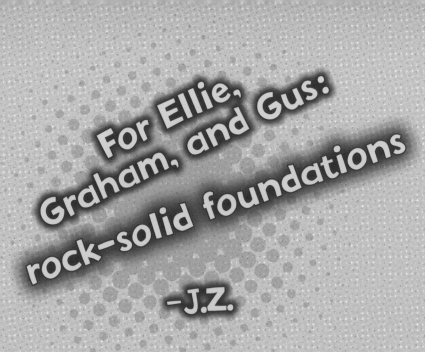

For Ellie,
Graham, and Gus:
rock-solid foundations

-J.Z.

Lerner Publications Company
A division of Lerner Publishing Group, Inc.
241 First Avenue North
Minneapolis, MN 55401 U.S.A.

Website address: www.lernerbooks.com

Library of Congress Cataloging-in-Publication Data

Zuehlke Jeffrey, 1968-
    The Hoover Dam / by Jeffrey Zuehlke.
        p.   cm. — (Lightning Bolt Books™—Famous Places)
    Includes index.
    ISBN 978-0-8225-9408-6 (lib. bdg. : alk. paper)
    1. Hoover Dam (Ariz. and Nev.)—History—Juvenile literature. I. Title.
    TC557.5.H6Z84 2010
    627'.820979313—dc22   2008031245

Manufactured in the United States of America
1 2 3 4 5 6 — BP — 15 14 13 12 11 10

Contents

A Dam Like No Other

Have you ever seen this structure? **This is Hoover Dam.**

Dams control rivers and streams. Hoover Dam is one of the largest dams in the world. It is very important. It sends power and water to many people.

Dams control water in rivers like this one.

Hoover Dam holds back the mighty **Colorado River.** It keeps the river from causing floods. The dam holds the water in a huge lake.

Hoover Dam slows the flow of the Colorado River. A lake lies behind the dam.

The lake is a reservoir (a place where water is held for later use). It is named Lake Mead. People use Lake Mead's water in many important ways.

Lake Mead is the largest man-made lake in the United States.

People use some of the
water in their homes.

What do you do with water?

Many homes
depend on Lake
Mead for water.

Farmers use Lake Mead's water for their crops. Watering crops is called irrigation.

What else does the Hoover Dam do?

Water from Lake Mead helps crops grow.

Hoover Dam makes electricity. Water runs through tunnels inside the dam. The water spins giant machines called generators.

This action creates hydroelectric power (power produced by moving water). The spinning generators create electricity for people to use.

Electricity created by the generators lights up Hoover Dam at night.

Where Is Hoover Dam?

Hoover Dam is in the southwestern United States.

It sits between the states of
Nevada and Arizona.

Lake Mead provides water to people in Utah, Nevada, Arizona, and California. The dam's generators also produce electricity for these people.

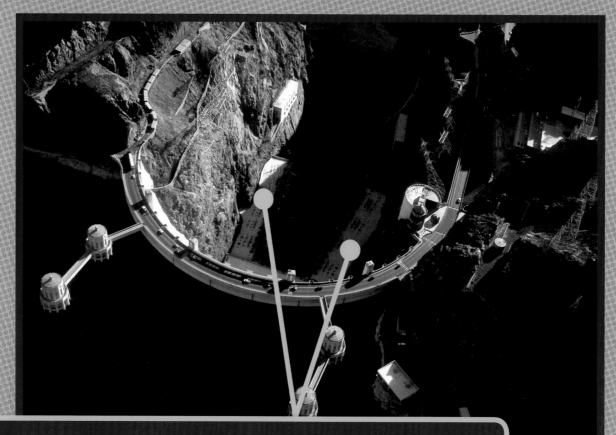

Hoover Dam's generators are inside two power plants (shown above). The power plants are at the base of the dam.

The area around the dam used to be dry desert. Very little rain falls near Lake Mead. People couldn't live or farm on the land.

Farmers in California tried to grow crops in the desert. But the land was too dry.

When water did come, there was too much of it!

Every spring, the Colorado River caused huge floods. It covered the land with water.

People stand on the roof of their house after floodwaters have covered their land.

But the water dried up too quickly. Farmers couldn't use it. So the U.S. government decided to build Hoover Dam to control the river's flow.

Building Hoover Dam

Building Hoover Dam was a huge job. No one had ever built such a large dam before.

Workers supported by ropes help build Hoover Dam.

Workers from all over the United States came to work on Hoover Dam.

More than five thousand people worked on the dam. They started in 1931. It took them five years to finish the job.

The workers needed a dry place to build the dam. So they decided to move the river! Workers cut four tunnels. The river water would flow through them.

Workers had to cut through rock to create the tunnels.

Workers blasted the rocky canyon walls with dynamite. Then they hauled the rock out. It took more than a year to finish the tunnels.

Workers had to finish the tunnels before work on the dam could begin.

The water flowed through the tunnels. Then the workers built structures called cofferdams. The cofferdams also helped stop water from getting into the building site. They helped hold back water so that workers could build on dry ground.

Dump trucks dropped loads of rocks in the river to make the cofferdams.

Next, workers had to make the canyon walls smooth. Men attached to ropes blasted the rock away. Then they smoothed out the canyon walls.

Workers dangle over the side of a cliff as they smooth the sides of the canyon walls.

Workers used concrete to build the dam. They poured the concrete into blocks. The blocks fit together like bricks on a house.

The dam is made of giant blocks of concrete.

Workers also built intake towers behind the dam. Intake towers allow water to go through the dam when people need it.

The Hoover Dam's four intake towers can be seen in this picture.

Workers built the generators below the dam too. When they finished, they closed the tunnels. Lake Mead began to form. The generators began to produce electricity.

This picture shows all the different parts of Hoover Dam.

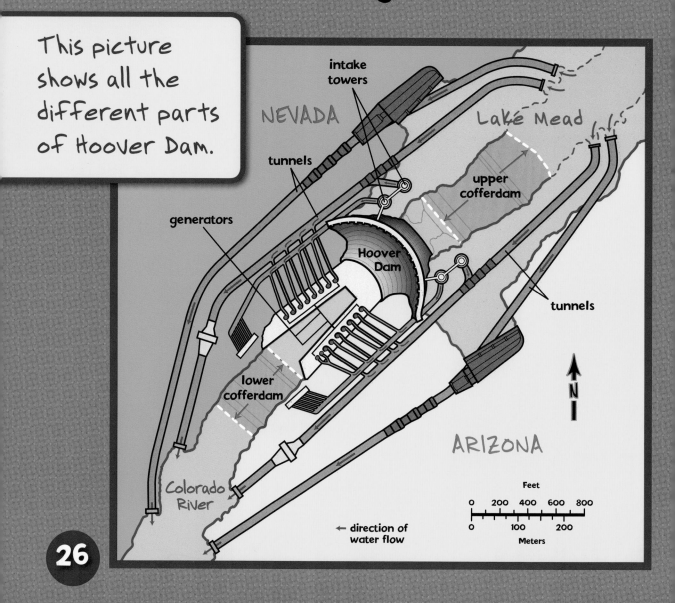

NEVADA

intake towers

Lake Mead

tunnels

generators

Hoover Dam

upper cofferdam

tunnels

lower cofferdam

Colorado River

ARIZONA

← direction of water flow

Feet
0   200 400 600 800

0   100   200
Meters

N

Hoover Dam is still working. It helps bring water and electricity to the southwest. Millions of people visit this beautiful structure every year.

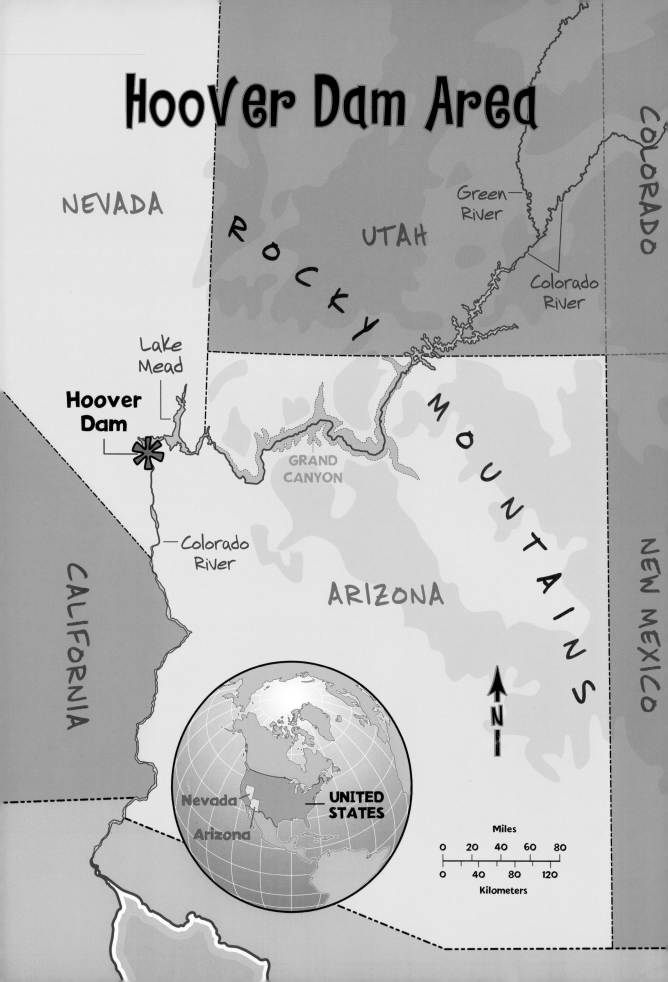

Hoover Dam Area

NEVADA

UTAH

COLORADO

ROCKY

Green
River

Colorado
River

Lake
Mead

**Hoover
Dam**

MOUNTAINS

GRAND
CANYON

Colorado
River

ARIZONA

CALIFORNIA

NEW MEXICO

N

Nevada

Arizona

UNITED
STATES

Miles

| 0 | 20 | 40 | 60 | 80 |

| 0 | 40 | 80 | 120 |

Kilometers

Fun Facts

- Hoover Dam is 725 feet (221 meters) high. That is about as tall as a sixty-story building.

- Hoover Dam creates electricity for about 1.3 million people in the states that surround it.

- The cement that workers used to create Hoover Dam would be enough to build a highway all the way from the Atlantic Ocean on the East Coast to the Pacific Ocean on the West Coast!

- Lake Mead is 8 miles (13 kilometers) wide at its widest point.

- Hoover Dam was named after Herbert Hoover, the thirty-first president of the United States. For a time, the dam was called Boulder Dam. It became Hoover Dam in 1947.

Glossary

cofferdam: a dam that is built to allow workers to build another larger dam on dry ground

concrete: a hard substance made from cement, sand, gravel, and water. Concrete is used for making roads, bridges, buildings, and dams.

dam: a structure that holds back water

dynamite: a special powder or material that can blow apart stone and other hard, strong things

electricity: a form of energy that lights lamps, heats houses, and makes refrigerators and other appliances work

generator: a machine that creates electricity

hydroelectric power: power produced by moving water. The moving water turns generators that create electricity.

irrigation: watering crops

reservoir: a holding area where water is stored for later use

structure: something that is built, such as a building, home, or dam

Further Reading

Building Big: Dam Basics
http://www.pbs.org/wgbh/buildingbig/dam/basics.html

Filbin, Dan. *Arizona*. Minneapolis: Lerner Publications Company, 2002.

Hoover Dam Website
http://www.usbr.gov/lc/hooverdam

Murray, Julie. *Hoover Dam*. Edina, MN: Abdo, 2005.

Sirvaitis, Karen. *Nevada*. Minneapolis: Lerner Publications Company, 2003.

Winget, Mary. *Floods*. Minneapolis: Lerner Publications Company, 2009.

Index

Photo Acknowledgments

The images in this book are used with the permission of: the Bureau of Reclamation, pp. 4, 18, 25, 27, 31; © age fotostock/SuperStock, p. 5; © Peter/Stef Lamberti/Stone/Getty Images, p. 6; © Mauritius/SuperStock, p. 7; © Adrian Green/Photographer's Choice/Getty Images, p. 8; Jeff Vanuga, USDA Natural Resources Conservation Service, p. 9; © Bryan Busovicki/Dreamstime.com, p. 10; © George Steinmetz/CORBIS, p. 11; © Stephen Simpson/Taxi/Getty Images, pp. 12–13; © Peter Frischmuth/Peter Arnold, Inc., p. 14; Library of Congress (LC-USZ62-127860), p. 15; Coachella Valley Museum and Cultural Center, pp. 16–17; Boulder City Museum and Historical Association, p. 19; National Archives, Rocky Mountain Region, pp. 20, 23; W. A. Bechtel Collection, University of Nevada, Las Vegas Libraries, Special Collections, pp. 21, 22, 24; © Laura Westlund/Independent Picture Service, pp. 26, 28.

Front cover: Bureau of Reclamation.